3 1603 20067 0416

TABLE of CONTENTS

D0763134

CHAPTER

CHAPTER ONE

INTRODUCING THE EMPIRE STATE

The Brooklyn Bridge has been a significant landmark in New York since its opening in 1883.

If you like variety, come to New York—the state that has everything. The diversity of New York's landscape, from the fruit and dairy-producing valleys to the rugged peaks of mountain ranges, is matched only by the variety of people who live and work in New York, as well as visit, each day.

The first people came to the land we now call New York about 10,000 years ago, and they haven't stopped coming since. The Dutch settlers called it New Netherland, after their homeland. It was also nicknamed the Knickerbocker State, after the style of pants the Dutch wore, called knickers. In 1664, the name was officially changed to New York in honor of England's Duke of York. When George Washington came to New York, he saw the state as the beginning of a great new world. He called New York the "seat of a new empire," which is how New York's official nickname became the Empire State.

New York has always attracted people of different backgrounds. In 1664, a Dutch minister remarked that more than 18 languages could be heard on the streets. More than 350 years later, that number has risen to several hundred. New York is the first stop for numerous immigrants (people arriving in the United States from other countries), many of whom decide to stay.

What comes to mind when you think of New York?

❖ New York City, the most populated city in the country and the cultural and financial capital of the world

❖ Sports fans cheering for New York's many professional sports teams

❖ Vineyards in the Finger Lakes region and on Long Island

❖ Adirondack Park, a natural playground for hiking, fishing, skiing, and more

❖ Milk, apples, and grapes, some of New York's chief farm products

❖ Workers producing snack foods and Pepsi-Cola in Purchase

❖ King Kong's favorite skyscraper—the Empire State Building

It's been said that, "If the United States is a melting pot, then New York makes it bubble." Read the story of this extraordinary state and its people, and you'll understand why they all love New York!

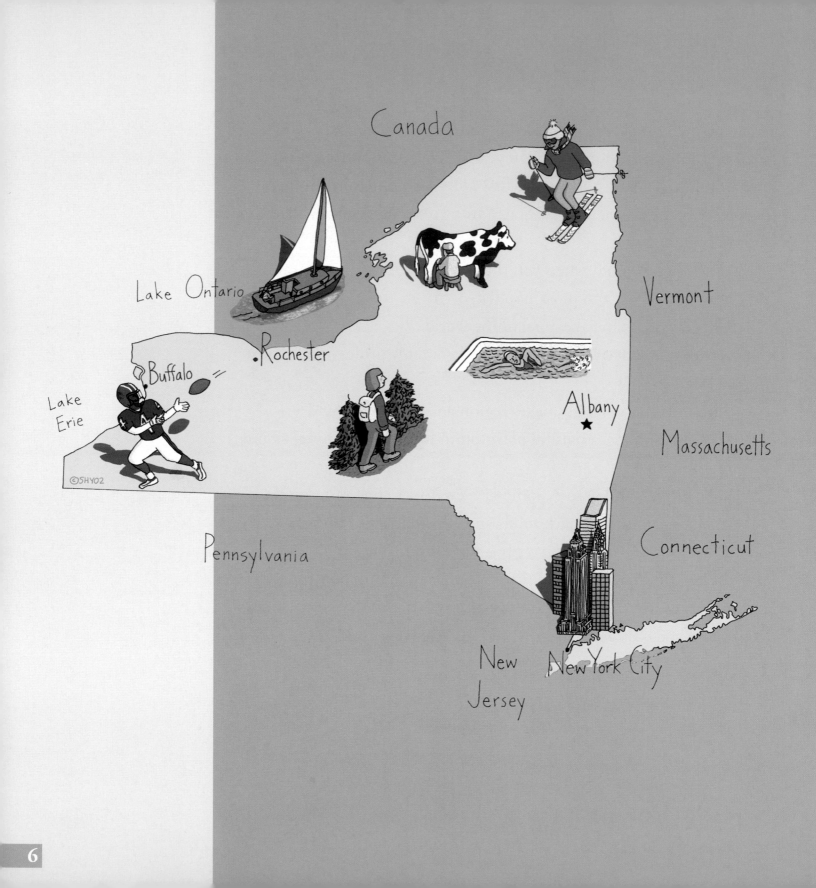

Canada

Lake Ontario

Lake Erie

Buffalo

Rochester

Vermont

Albany

Massachusetts

Pennsylvania

Connecticut

New York City

New Jersey

©SHY02

CHAPTER TWO

THE LAND OF NEW YORK

New York is a Mid-Atlantic state, which means that it is in the middle of the Atlantic coastline. New York shares its eastern border with Vermont, Massachusetts, and Connecticut. The state also shares a water border with Rhode Island to the east. Lake Ontario and Lake Erie shape New York's western border, along with part of another country, Canada, which also lies to the north. New Jersey and Pennsylvania make up New York's southern border, and the Atlantic Ocean borders Long Island.

The total area of New York is 54,556 square miles (141,299 square kilometers), making it the 27th largest state in the country. At its widest point, New York stretches 320 miles (515 kilometers) east to west, not including Long Island. Its longest stretch north to south covers 310 miles (499 km).

You can get a great view of the Adirondack region from this trail stairway on Whiteface Mountain.

Much of New York's land was formed thousands of years ago, during an era known as the Ice Age. At this time, much of the area we now call New York was covered with thick sheets of ice called glaciers. The glaciers moved from north to south, digging valleys and flattening mountains to create high, level stretches of land called plateaus. Glaciers also cut away existing plateaus, leaving behind rocky peaks.

This glacier activity helped to make the land of New York what it is today. There are eight land regions in New York: the Adirondack Region, the Tug Hill Plateau, the St. Lawrence–Lake Champlain Lowland, the Appalachian/Allegheny Plateau, the Erie–Ontario Lowland, the Hudson–Mohawk Lowland, the New England Upland, and the Atlantic Coastal Plain.

Adirondack Region

The Adirondack region covers 26,000 square miles (67,340 sq km) in the northeastern part of the state. This area is covered with deep forests. It is the highest and most rugged land in New York.

In this region you will find the Adirondack Mountains. The Adirondacks were formed one billion years ago, when tectonic plates pushed against each other, forcing the land upwards. Tectonic plates are pieces of the earth, deep down, that shift and move. The highest peak in the Adirondacks (and in the state) is Mount Marcy, which rises 5,344 feet (1,630 meters) above sea level.

To protect this rugged, beautiful land, New York set aside 6 million acres in 1892 as a wilderness preserve called Adirondack Park. Trees

such as hemlock, pine, and spruce cover the Adirondacks within the park's 3,900 square miles (10,101 sq km) of preserved forests. This area is enjoyed by vacationers from around the world.

The Adirondack Mountains are a popular destination for nature lovers.

Tug Hill Plateau

This flat, rocky area is north of Oneida Lake and separated from the Adirondack region by the Black River Valley. Winter storms picking up moisture from Lake Ontario routinely drop more than 225

EXTRA! EXTRA!

Adirondack Park is the largest park in the continental United States. It is about the same size as New York's neighbor, Vermont, and it is larger than the Yosemite, Yellowstone, Grand Canyon, and Glacier national parks combined.

inches (572 centimeters) of snow there every year. It is the least settled area of New York because the soil is too poor for farming, and the weather is so harsh.

St. Lawrence–Lake Champlain Lowland

The St. Lawrence–Lake Champlain Lowland rolls along the southern bank of the St. Lawrence River and around the eastern bank of Lake Champlain. This land is ideal for farming due to the fertile soil of the riverbank.

In this region you'll find the Thousand Islands, a group of about 1,800 islands and 3,000 shoals. Shoals are sandy mounds rising up from the bottom of the river. The islands vary in size from mere points of rock to several square miles in area. The region is a popular vacation spot, and many people also call the islands home.

Several bridges connect the Thousand Islands.

Appalachian/Allegheny Plateau

Half of New York is located in the Appalachian Plateau, the largest land region in the state. The fertile lands of this region are found around the Finger Lakes and in the valleys of rivers emptying from the Catskill Mountains. The land supports dairy farms, vegetable farms, vineyards, and nurseries.

The rugged parts of this region include the Catskill, Shawangunk, and Allegheny mountains. At one time, the Catskill Mountains were not mountains. They were part of a high, level plain, or plateau. Over thousands of years, glaciers cut away these plateaus, creating peaks. Today, the Catskills are a popular recreation area, and its reservoirs provide most of New York City's fresh water. At the southern end of the Catskills are the Shawangunk Mountains. They are long and narrow, and continue into New Jersey and Pennsylvania. To the north and west of the Catskills are the Allegheny Mountains.

The Catskill Forest Preserve is 300,000 acres (121,500 ha) of protected springs, waterfalls, forests, and wildlife.

Lake Erie–Ontario Lowland

The low, flat plains of this region lie along the southern shores of Lakes Erie and Ontario, stretching north of the Appalachian Plateau to the western side of the Mohawk River Valley. There are many swamps in

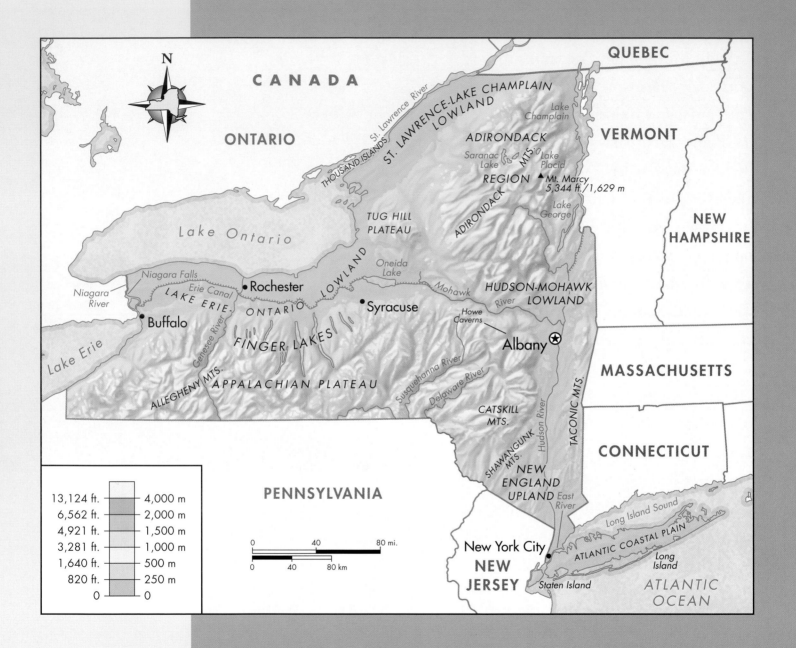

N

QUEBEC

CANADA

ONTARIO

St. Lawrence River

THOUSAND ISLANDS

ST. LAWRENCE-LAKE CHAMPLAIN
LOWLAND

Lake Champlain

VERMONT

ADIRONDACK

Saranac Lake

ADIRONDACK MTS.

Lake Placid

REGION ▲ Mt. Marcy
5,344 ft./1,629 m

ADIRONDACK

Lake George

NEW HAMPSHIRE

Lake Ontario

TUG HILL PLATEAU

ONTARIO LOWLAND

Oneida Lake

Mohawk River

HUDSON-MOHAWK LOWLAND

Niagara Falls

Erie Canal

• Rochester

Niagara River

LAKE ERIE-

Genesee River

ONTARIO

• Syracuse

Howe Caverns

Albany ✪

• Buffalo

FINGER LAKES

Lake Erie

ALLEGHENY MTS.

APPALACHIAN PLATEAU

Susquehanna River

Delaware River

CATSKILL MTS.

Hudson River

TACONIC MTS.

MASSACHUSETTS

CONNECTICUT

SHAWANGUNK MTS.

NEW ENGLAND UPLAND

East River

Long Island Sound

PENNSYLVANIA

13,124 ft.	4,000 m
6,562 ft.	2,000 m
4,921 ft.	1,500 m
3,281 ft.	1,000 m
1,640 ft.	500 m
820 ft.	250 m
0	0

0   40   80 mi.

0   40   80 km

New York City

NEW JERSEY

Staten Island

ATLANTIC COASTAL PLAIN

Long Island

ATLANTIC OCEAN

this area, as well as drumlins. Drumlins are oval-shaped mounds of earth and stone from 50 to 200 feet (15 to 61 m) high.

Hudson–Mohawk Lowland

The Hudson–Mohawk Lowland includes the valleys along the Hudson and Mohawk rivers, between the Catskill, Adirondack, and Taconic mountains. This region is only about 10 to 30 miles (16 to 48 km) wide.

Howe Caverns, near Albany, is one of the coolest places in the Hudson–Mohawk Lowland—literally! This cavern, or large cave, was formed when an ancient, underground stream carved through layers of limestone. The cave is 156 feet (48 m) underground and has a river along its floor. Because it is underground, the temperature in the cave is always a cool 52° Fahrenheit (11° Celsius). Water still trickles in, slowly changing the walls, ceiling, and floor of the cave. As water seeps into the soil, it picks up small amounts of limestone. When the water reaches the cave, it evaporates, depositing the limestone inside the cave.

Howe Caverns is located 156 feet (48 m)—about 15 stories—underground.

EXTRA! EXTRA!

Mineral deposits that hang from the ceiling of a cave are called *stalactites*. Deposits that rise from the floor are called *stalagmites*. *Flowstone* is formed when limestone is deposited along the cave walls.

New England Upland

The New England Upland lies east of the Hudson River, along the lower half of New York's eastern border. It includes the southern part of the Hudson River Valley and Manhattan Island. In this region you'll find some of the oldest mountains in North America, the Taconic Mountains, which rise 2,000 feet (610 m). The Taconic Mountains are part of the Appalachian Mountain range, which runs from Quebec, Canada, to the state of Alabama.

Along the west bank of the Hudson River, near the town of Haverstraw, there's a 14-mile (23-km) stretch of cliffs called the Palisades. The Palisades were formed 200 million years ago by a great sheet of magma, a fiery material under Earth's crust that turned into rock when it cooled. The land was pushed up, much like when mountains form, and erosion of the land exposed the cliffs.

Atlantic Coastal Plain

Long Island and Staten Island make up the Atlantic Coastal Plain. Farms in this area are successful in growing vegetables, fruit, and flowers, and raising poultry. The shores of Long Island attract many beach lovers, and the waters of the coast are great for fishing. The breezes from these waters moderate the temperature along the northern and southern forks of Long Island, making them ideal places for vineyards. The Great

South Bay off Long Island is the leading harvest area of hard clams in the United States.

Fire Island, on the south shore of Long Island, is a beach-lovers' haven.

RIVERS AND LAKES

New York rivers and lakes act as trade and transportation routes. They also form borders and provide recreation spots for swimming, boating, and fishing. Many New York rivers also played important roles in the development of the state.

The Delaware, Susquehanna, Allegheny, and Hudson rivers are four of New York's largest. The Delaware forms New York's southwestern border with Pennsylvania and is a favorite for fishing and canoeing. The Susquehanna flows from Otsego Lake, northeast of Binghamton, into Pennsylvania. The Allegheny starts near Pittsburgh, Pennsylvania, and loops north into western New York before flowing back into Pennsylvania.

The state's longest and most important river, the Hudson, flows more than 300 miles (483 km) past the cities of Albany and West Point, and the cliffs of the Palisades. Near the tip of Manhattan Island, it flows into New York Bay before emptying into the Atlantic Ocean. Along this journey, more than 150 tributary streams flow into the Hudson. In the lower Hudson River Valley, the Hudson becomes an estuary when its fresh water mixes with the salt water of the Atlantic Ocean.

The Hudson is one of America's great rivers.

The powerful Niagara River flows 34 miles (55 km) from Lake Erie into Lake Ontario. Along the way it falls over the Niagara Escarpment, creating one of New York's most breathtaking natural landmarks, Niagara Falls. The escarpment is the eroded edge of an ancient sea floor that rose up 245 million years ago. The falls are only partially in New York; the rest lies in Canada. The 182-foot (55-m) American Falls is high— but not the highest in New York. Taughannock Falls in the Finger Lake region is higher, at 215 feet (66 m).

New York has about 7,500 lakes and ponds. The state's largest lakes are Lakes Erie and Ontario, which lie along the border with Canada. A portion of both lakes lies within the New York state border. The Finger Lakes, eleven long lakes that are shaped like the fingers of a hand, are located in the western part of the state. Each lake is named after an Iroquois tribe: Canandaigua, Keuka, Seneca, Cayuga, Owasco, Skaneateles, Conesus, Hemlock, Canadice, Honeoye, and Otisco.

Visitors can get a close-up look at the American Falls from Goat Island.

FIND OUT MORE

The Niagara River is used to produce hydroelectric power, or electricity that is produced by the movement of flowing water. Up to 375,000 gallons of water per second are diverted from the Niagara River just before it goes over Niagara Falls. The water is then moved through underground canals to machines called turbines, where the movement of the water spins the turbines. How do these spinning turbines produce electricity?

Northeast of the Finger Lakes is Oneida Lake, New York's largest natural inland lake. In the Adirondack region there are more than 2,000 lakes and ponds, including Lake George, Saranac Lake, and Lake Placid, home of the 1932 and 1980 Winter Olympics. Lake Champlain is 107 miles (172 km) long and forms part of New York's eastern border with Vermont.

The Olympic ski jump complex in Lake Placid is used by professional ski jumpers for practice runs.

CLIMATE

Upstate New York generally has cooler weather than the coast, with average temperatures in the Adirondacks at 14°F (–10°C) in January and 66°F (19°C) in July. On Long Island, temperatures average 30°F (–1°C) in January and 74°F (23°C) in July.

The state gets an average of 32 to 58 inches (81 to 147 cm) of precipitation—rain and snow—every year. The central, northern, and western parts of the state have many large bodies of water that fill the air with moisture. As a result, cities such as Syracuse, Buffalo, and Rochester experience many cloudy days and greater snowfall than the rest of the state.

Residents of Saranac Lake celebrate winter by building an Ice Palace, made from 1,500 blocks of ice.

CHAPTER THREE

NEW YORK THROUGH HISTORY

Shown above is a detail of the painting *Colonial Days in New York City.*

The first inhabitants in North America were prehistoric people called Paleo-Indians. Scientists believe they arrived on this continent 15,000 to 35,000 years ago during the Ice Age, when much of the land was covered with glaciers. Paleo-Indians hunted large, prehistoric animals such as the mammoth for food, clothing, and shelter. When the Ice Age ended around 8000 B.C., new plants started to grow and animals evolved. The people adapted to their new environment by hunting smaller animals and gathering plants for food. This is known as the Archaic culture.

Over time, Native Americans began to settle in one area instead of roaming, and they started to grow crops. This is how the Eastern Woodland culture began. Eastern Woodland Indians could be found along the eastern coast from Canada to Florida.

The descendants of Eastern Woodland Indians were Algonquian-speaking tribes. These tribes formed in many parts of North America, including present-day New York. The Mahicans settled along the upper banks of the Hudson River, north to Lake Champlain. The Wappinger tribe lived southeast of the Mahicans, along the Hudson, from Poughkeepsie to Manhattan Island. The Lenni-Lenape lived in southeastern New York, on Manhattan Island, and on the western end of Long Island. They also lived in what is now New Jersey, Delaware, and eastern Pennsylvania. English settlers referred to the Lenape as Delawares, because they lived near the Delaware River.

These Native Americans fished and hunted, and gathered nuts, berries, and roots. They also grew corn. For shelter, they drove small trees into the ground about 2 feet (.6 m) apart, to form either a circle or a rectangle. The tops of the poles were tied together with vines or strips of bark, which were also used to cover the framework.

Around A.D. 1300, Iroquois-speaking tribes formed in New York. They lived between the northern Hudson River and the Genesee River.

Native Americans hunted deer for food.

This drawing shows a Mohawk village in the early days of New York.

These tribes included the Mohawk, Oneida, Onondaga, Cayuga, and Seneca. They built longhouses out of trees, bark, and woven grasses. Each village had several longhouses, with each house holding 10 to 15 families. For protection, the Iroquois surrounded their villages with a high fence made of logs. Each tribe worked as a group. Men hunted and fished, and women tended to the crops of corn, beans, squash, and tobacco. Iroquois tribes also traded with one another. They established trade routes throughout New York, many of which were later used as the state's first paved roads.

Not all the Iroquois tribes got along, and for 300 years they fought over land. In 1570, an Onondaga chief named Hiawatha united five Iroquois tribes: the Seneca, Cayuga, Onondaga, Oneida, and the Mohawk. They called their new group the League of the Great Peace. It is also referred to as the League of Five Nations, or the Iroquois Confederacy. This group helped the tribes to work out their differences peacefully. Around 1715, the Tuscarora joined the confederacy, making it the League of Six Nations. Each group still lived by their own rules, but a tribal council settled arguments between the groups. Their government leaders were chosen by the people. It was the first democracy in North America.

EUROPEAN EXPLORERS

In the 1500s, European countries traded goods with Asia. To make trading easier, they tried to find faster trading routes to Asia by sailing west. In 1524, Italian explorer Giovanni da Verrazzano sailed into New York Bay in search of this route. He was sent by King Francis I of France. He didn't stay long, however; he was driven out by stormy weather.

Other explorers looking for this route also found North America. This new land was exciting, and more explorers came and began trading with Native Americans there. The Europeans were especially interested in beaver pelts, or fur, which was in great demand at the time. Beavers were plentiful in North America.

In 1603, Samuel de Champlain came to North America from France as part of a fur-trading trip to Canada. In 1609, Champlain traveled south from Canada and explored the lake in northeastern New York that now bears his name. That same year, Henry Hudson, an Englishman employed by the Dutch, also sailed to North America in search of a trade route. Hudson sailed into New York Bay and up the river that is now named for him.

In 1609, Henry Hudson sailed up the Hudson River in his ship, the *Half Moon*.

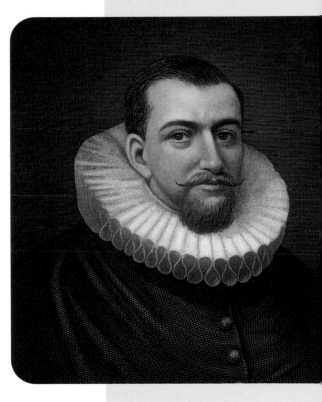

Although Hudson didn't find the route he was looking for, he found something even better—New York Bay. The bay was a natural harbor, and trade ships sailing there would be safe from the rough waters of the ocean. The Dutch quickly set up trading posts along the Hudson River. In exchange for pelts, they traded European goods with the Native Americans.

Peter Minuit purchased the island of Manhattan from Native Americans.

NEW NETHERLAND

The Dutch were successful in the fur trade. In 1624, the Dutch West India Company sent about 25 families from the Netherlands to establish a colony along the Hudson River. They named this land New Netherland, and their settlement Fort Orange (later called Albany). Some colonists lived at the mouth of the river, on Manhattan Island. They called this town New Amsterdam. Legend says that in 1626, Peter Minuit, the colony's first director (governor), bought Manhattan Island from the Lenni-Lenape tribe for 60 Dutch guilders (worth about $24) of beads and trinkets.

While the first colonists were from the Netherlands, New Amsterdam welcomed people from many different countries. By the 1640s, colonists spoke more than 18 languages, including French, English, Swedish, Danish, and German. Many settlers were merchants in the fur trade, but others worked as tavernkeepers, doctors, and artisans.

The Dutch settlers got along well with the Iroquois. The Iroquois, however, were constantly battling with Algonquians over land. Willem Kieft, the governor of New Netherland in 1638, favored the Iroquois. In what is sometimes referred to as Governor Kieft's War, Kieft repeatedly attacked the Algonquians between 1640 and 1645. Many lives were lost on both sides. It wasn't long before Kieft was removed as governor.

In 1647, the Dutch sent Peter Stuyvesant to be the governor of New Amsterdam. He was strict, but honest. He cleaned and improved the streets, regulated the value of wampum, a form of money, and started a public school system. He also ended the fighting with Native Americans. As a result, more families moved to New Amsterdam, and the colony's population grew. By the 1660s there were 9,000 men, women, and children calling New Amsterdam home.

EXTRA! EXTRA!

Native American tribes along the East Coast made beads from shells. These beads, or *wampum*, were strung together and used as money to trade with Europeans in the 1600s. Native Americans also used wampum in sacred rituals.

The Dutch weren't the only Europeans establishing colonies in North America. England had settlements in Massachusetts and Connecticut. In an effort to expand their colony, English settlers in Connecticut seized land on Long Island, claiming it for England. In 1664, British (English) troops arrived to claim the rest of southern New York. The townspeople did not want a war, so Peter Stuyvesant peacefully surrendered New Amsterdam. Fort Orange was claimed by the British ten years later. The British changed the names of New Amsterdam and Fort Orange to New York and Albany, after the Duke of York and Albany.

Peter Stuyvesant peacefully surrendered New Amsterdam to the British.

NEW YORK BORDERS

When the king of England gave the colony to the Duke of York, its boundary stretched from the Connecticut River in the east to the Delaware River in the west. This included all of present-day New York, New Jersey, and Vermont, as well as the western half of Connecticut.

Meanwhile, the neighboring colony of New Hampshire wanted to expand westward. In 1749, the governor of New Hampshire began to issue titles to land west of the Connecticut River. These were called the New Hampshire Land Grants. However, New York had issued titles in the same area, and they would not acknowledge New Hampshire's claim. In 1770, a man named Ethan Allen gathered a small army called the Green Mountain Boys (named after the surrounding mountains) to drive New Yorkers out of this territory. His small but fierce army was successful, and New York ultimately gave up control of this area, which later became the state of Vermont.

FAMOUS FIRSTS

- The country's first railroad ran 11 miles (18 km) between Albany and Schenectady and opened August 9, 1831.
- The first billionaire, John Davison Rockefeller, was born in Richford in 1839.
- The first complete American mastodon skeleton was found in Newburgh in 1845.
- The first landscaped public park in the country was Central Park, opened in 1859.
- The first firehouse pole was installed by Captain David B. Kenyon of Engine Company #21 in New York City on April 21, 1878.
- New York was the first state to require license plates on cars in 1901.
- The country's first permanent coast-to-coast radio network, NBC, was established in New York City in 1926.

FRENCH AND INDIAN WARS

From the late 1600s to the mid 1700s, England and France fought a series of wars to gain control of North America. Much of the French

MINERAL COUNTY LIBRARY
PO BOX 1390
HAWTHORNE, NV 89415

and Indian War (1754–1763) was fought in New York, where the Iroquois tribes sided with the British, and the Algonquian tribes sided with the French. In 1759, the British took Fort Carillon away from the French and renamed it Fort Ticonderoga. The British also took control of French Forts Niagara and Crown Point. In the end, the British held claim to land in the northern and southern parts of present-day New York.

The British fought for control of Fort Ticonderoga because of its strategic location near Lake Champlain.

THE AMERICAN REVOLUTION

To help pay for the French and Indian war, Britain needed to raise money. To do this, the British government passed strict trading laws for all of its colonies, including New York, and imposed high taxes (extra charges) on things people bought. One of these new taxes was the Stamp Act of 1765, which applied to all printed material, such as newspapers.

The colonists resented the taxes. Because they didn't have a voice in the British government, they didn't feel it was fair for Britain to tax them. The colonists protested, and the Stamp Act was repealed the following year. For many colonists, getting the Stamp Act repealed was only the first step. They wanted complete freedom from British rule. These people were called Patriots.

The conflict between the colonies and Britain ultimately led to a war for independence, called the American Revolution (1775–1783). New Yorkers participated in several battles. On August 27, 1776, the British attacked Patriots

Colonists in New York protested the Stamp Act.

WHAT'S IN A NAME?

Some names of places in New York have interesting origins.

Name	Comes From or Means
Manhattan	Named after a Native American tribe that lived in the southern tip of New York State
Ellis Island	New York bought this island from the estate of Samuel Ellis
Genesee	Iroquois for "beautiful valley"
Poughkeepsie	Algonquian for "reed-covered lodge by the little water place"
Yonkers	From *jonker* which means "his young lordship" in Dutch; it was the title of Adriaen Cornelisen Van der Donck, who settled in the Yonkers area
Coxsackie	Algonquian for "hoot of an owl"
Ticonderoga	Iroquois for "the place between two waters"

defending Long Island and drove them north to Brooklyn Heights. By the time George Washington's army arrived the next day, more than 1,000 of his men had been captured.

Washington knew his small army couldn't defeat the thousands of British troops. Instead, Washington led his soldiers north from Brooklyn Heights. In the middle of a rainy night, they secretly crossed the East River to Manhattan. They moved north, losing men at battles in Harlem and White Plains. Washington rallied his troops, and in the winter of 1776 he moved his army into New Jersey, where he won battles in Trenton and Princeton. In 1783 the war came to an end. The colonists had finally won their freedom, and the United States was born.

On July 26, 1788, New York became the eleventh state to join the Union. George Washington became the nation's first president in 1789. He was inaugurated in New York City, which served as the nation's capital from 1785 to 1790. It was also the state's capital until 1797, when the capital moved to Albany.

The war weakened the Iroquois, who had sided with the British. Between 1784 and 1790, tribes of the Six Nations signed away most of their land in

With much fanfare, George Washington arrived in New York for his inauguration at Federal Hall.

exchange for money and help from the state. The Iroquois Confederacy was gone, and many of its former members moved to Canada. Some stayed in New York and lived on reservations, or lands set aside by the government specifically for their use.

Today, the Onondaga and Oneida live in central New York near Syracuse; the Tuscarora, Tonawanda, Cattaraugus, Allegany, and Oil Springs reservations are in western New York; and the St. Regis–Mohawk Reservation is located on the Canadian border. There are also two state reservations in New York—the Poospatuck and the Shinnecock on Long Island. (A federal reservation is recognized by the United States government, and a state reservation is recognized only by the state government).

WAR OF 1812

As the United States was forming its own, independent country, Britain and France were at war. They each tried to block the other from trading with fellow European countries. The British navy blocked French ports, which affected trade in the United States. As a result, in 1812 the United States joined the war, becoming involved in yet another conflict with Britain. Although only two battles were

I WANT YOU for the U.S. ARMY ENLIST NOW

EXTRA! EXTRA!

Uncle Sam (shown right) is a popular character that symbolizes the government of the United States. Many people think that Uncle Sam was based on a real person named Sam Wilson. Wilson was a meatpacker in Troy, New York. During the War of 1812, he stamped "U.S. Beef" on the meat that was sent to soldiers. The soldiers joked that the "U.S." stood for "Uncle Sam."

fought in New York, the United States defeated the British at each one. Both were naval battles, fought on Lake Erie and Lake Champlain.

THE NEW YORK STOCK EXCHANGE

FIND OUT MORE

The telegraph, the stock ticker, and the telephone were invented in the 1800s. How did these inventions help the New York Stock Exchange grow?

Since the early days of New Amsterdam, merchants and traders had been buying and selling goods on what is today called Wall Street. After the American Revolution, stocks and bonds were also bought and sold. Bonds were issued by the government to help pay the costs of the war. A *bond* is a document indicating that someone has loaned money to the government. The government promises to pay that person back—with interest—at a later date. If a person owns *stock* in a company, it means that he or she owns part of that company. The more successful the company, the more its stock is worth. The Bank of New York, as well as other companies, began selling stock to help expand their business.

The people who handled this kind of trading were called brokers. In 1792, a group of 24 brokers created what was known as the stock exchange. In 1817, the exchange adopted a constitution, or a system of laws, and became the New York Stock and Exchange Board.

A GROWING STATE

During the early 1800s, many people moved to central and western New York. Some came from other parts of the state. Others moved there from New Jersey, Delaware, and Canada. Many settlers were attracted

by the region's fertile soil. By 1820, about half-a-million people had moved into the New York area.

New Yorkers gathered in Battery Park in the early 1800s.

To handle the increase in population, better transportation was needed. In 1797, the first paved roadway ran between Albany and Schenectady. The first railroad was also built between these towns in 1831.

The most important transportation development of this time was the Erie Canal. Governor De Witt Clinton wanted to create a waterway

The first barges from Buffalo arrive in New York City via the Erie Canal.

connecting the Hudson River with Lake Erie in order to ship goods from New York to the rest of the country. Many people thought it couldn't be done. They nicknamed the canal "Clinton's Big Ditch." In spite of this, the Erie Canal was built between 1817 and 1825. The canal was 363 miles long (584 km) and 40 feet (12 m) wide. Mules walked on towpaths alongside the canal, pulling the boats.

To everyone's surprise, Clinton's idea worked. The canal made it easier, faster, and cheaper to transport farm produce, industrial products, and settlers to and from New York City and into the western frontier. Towns such as Utica, Syracuse, Rochester, and Buffalo built up quickly along the canal.

Between 1825 and 1855, New York's population doubled, and New York City's population quadrupled. Most of the new-comers were from northern and western Europe. Rising rents and failing potato crops in Ireland brought thousands of Irish people to New York. By 1860 there were more than 200,000 Irish living in New York City. Many German immigrants settled in Rochester and Buffalo. In 1855, 74,000 people were living in Buffalo and 30,000 of them were German.

EXTRA! EXTRA!

The canal proved to be a cheaper method of transportation. Sending a ton of freight from Buffalo to New York City cost only $6 along the canal, compared to $100 before it was built. The canal was faster, too. A trip from Lake Erie to Albany, which once took more than a month, could be made in just seven days along the canal.

A group of Russian immigrants debark in New York.

Not everyone came to New York by choice. Since the time of the Dutch settlers, people from Africa and the West Indies were captured and brought to New York and the other colonies to work as slaves. Slaves were forced to do hard labor on farms, especially in the South. They were considered property, and were bought and sold between landowners. Slaves did not have the freedom to go where they wanted, and they were often treated poorly.

Efforts to abolish, or end, slavery in New York had begun as early as 1781, when New York freed all slaves who had served in the military.

These newly freed slaves could own land, but they could not vote. In 1799, the Gradual Emancipation Act was passed. It said that every male slave born after July 4, 1799 would be freed when he turned 28. (For women, the age was 24.) Little by little, slaves and former slaves gained more rights. By 1827, slavery was abolished in New York.

Although it was illegal to own a slave in New York, people still owned slaves in other parts of the

WHO'S WHO IN NEW YORK?

Sojourner Truth (1797?–1883), born Isabella Baumfree, worked as a slave in New Paltz. After gaining her freedom in 1828, she moved to New York City. In 1843 she changed her name to Sojourner Truth and began preaching the word of God. Her moving speeches against slavery inspired people all over the world. She was born in Ulster County.

country, particularly the South. Many people spoke out against slavery. These people were called abolitionists. Some abolitionists helped slaves escape to the North, where they could be free. Harriet Tubman, an escaped slave, lived for many years in Auburn. She helped others to escape along the Underground Railroad, a secret network of people and hiding places. Slaves moved at night and hid during the day. The places they hid were called stations, and the people who hid them were called conductors. Other New York abolitionists were Sojourner Truth, a former slave, and Horace Greeley, founder of the *New York Tribune*. Greeley wrote antislavery columns that had a great effect on many readers.

Elizabeth Cady Stanton and Lucretia Mott were abolitionists who also spoke out for women's rights. They wanted women to have the same rights as men. This included suffrage, which is the right to vote. In 1848, they organized the first Women's Rights Convention in the United States at Seneca Falls. In 1869, Stanton and Susan B. Anthony formed the National Woman Suffrage Association, an organization that worked to give women the right to vote. New York granted women the right to vote in 1917. Three years later, an amendment to the United States Constitution gave all women the right to vote.

FIND OUT MORE

Caroline Cowles Richards was a schoolgirl in Canandaigua, New York when she heard Susan B. Anthony speak about suffrage for women. In December 1855, Caroline wrote about the experience in her diary. ". . . She talked very plainly about our rights and how we ought to stand up for them, and said the world would never go right until the women had just as much right to vote and rule as the men." Diaries and letters from long ago offer a way to learn about history. Start your own journal and write about an important event in your life.

Elizabeth Cady Stanton was one of the most well-known leaders for women's rights.

Onlookers cheer as Union troops leave for war.

FIND OUT MORE

In 1861, eleven southern states left the Union and formed the Confederacy. Almost 300 years earlier, Chief Hiawatha brought five Iroquois tribes together to form the Iroquois Confederacy. How were these two groups alike? How were they different?

THE CIVIL WAR

Although women were gaining their rights, African Americans continued to struggle. During the 1800s, states in the South relied heavily on slave labor, because farming was a major part of southern life. The northern states had farms, but they were also building other industries. They didn't need slaves to keep their economy strong. The North wanted to end slavery in the United States, but the South believed each state had the right to decide for themselves. The conflict worsened until, in 1861, eleven southern states seceded, or withdrew, from the United States. They joined together to form a new nation called the Confederate States of America. This division between the North (the Union) and the South (the Confederacy) led to the Civil War (1861–1865).

Many New Yorkers were drafted into the Union army, which meant they had to fight or risk being arrested. Wealthy New Yorkers, however, could avoid fighting by paying $300. Those who could not afford to buy their way out of the war resented being forced to fight. They knew that the war could bring slavery to an end, and that newly freed slaves might then move north to compete for their jobs. Out of fear and anger, many people in New York City started a riot. For three days in July 1863, they broke into stores and burned houses. It was one of the worst riots in our country's history.

New York sent more than 460,000 soldiers to fight for the Union, more than any other state. New York also provided the greatest amount of money and supplies. Cold Spring, Ilion, and Watervliet made cannons, rifles, and ammunition. Schenectady made locomotives, and Troy made horseshoes. Mills all over the state made uniforms. All of these supplies were sent to soldiers along New York's rivers, canals, and railroads. The war came to an end in 1865, with the North victorious.

GILDED AGE

After the Civil War, industry and business in New York continued to grow. This period of great wealth, which lasted into the 1920s, is known as the Gilded Age. (*Gilded* means "covered with gold.") During this time, many businessmen became millionaires. Some New York millionaires were John D. Rockefeller, Cornelius Vanderbilt, and John Pierpont Morgan. Rockefeller owned the Standard Oil Company, and J. P. Morgan owned United States Steel. Vanderbilt started the Staten Island Ferry when he was just sixteen years old. He also made a tremendous fortune building railroads. These millionaires built mansions and summer homes along the Hudson River and on Long Island.

Not everyone in New York was rich. Life was especially hard on immigrants. By 1892, almost all immigrants passed though the immigra-

John D. Rockefeller, a native of New York, was once one of the richest men in the country.

On March 25, 1911, fire engulfed the Triangle Shirtwaist Company.

tion center at Ellis Island. Between 1890 and 1900, the population of New York City went from 1,525,301 to 3,437,202. This flood of immigrants arrived mainly from Ireland, Italy, and Eastern Europe. Some worked as craftsmen in expanding industries. Others tried their hand in chemical and electrical industries.

It was difficult for immigrant families to support themselves in New York City. Factory conditions were poor, hours were long, and people were paid very little. Sometimes children as young as six worked in factories to help their family. In 1911, a fire broke out at a New York City factory called the Triangle Shirtwaist Company. Many workers were trapped inside because stairwell doors were locked, and halls and aisles were blocked with cloth, baskets, and machinery. More than 140 factory workers were killed, most of whom were young girls between the ages of sixteen and twenty-three.

As a result of this terrible fire, an organization called the Factory Investigating Commission was set up to inspect factories across the state. By 1914, New York had passed new labor laws. These laws brought better working conditions, fair wages, and restrictions on child labor.

THE HARLEM RENAISSANCE

During the early 1900s, many African Americans from the South began moving into New York. They settled in Harlem, which became the largest and most influential African-American community in the nation. African-American musicians brought jazz to New York. They called New York City "The Big Apple" because playing music for audiences there meant they had made it big.

THE GREAT DEPRESSION

The great wealth of the 1920s was not shared equally. Many people spent more money than they earned. So much was produced—food, cars, appliances, and other things—that there weren't enough people to buy it all. This made the economy unstable. More and more people invested in the stock market, hoping to get rich.

On October 29, 1929, the stock market crashed. Company stocks lost their value, and people who owned stocks lost a lot of money. Many businesses closed, and thousands of people across the country lost their jobs, homes, and savings. Without jobs, people could not afford to buy the things they needed, including food. This difficult time is known as the Great Depression (1929–1939).

In 1930, the city of Rochester offered jobs to people who needed them. Jobs included building and repairing roads, schools, and other public works. Soon Buffalo and New York City did the same. Governor Franklin Delano Roosevelt created the Temporary Relief Emergency Administration. This program gave jobs to those who could work, and money to those who needed to buy food. When Roosevelt became president of the United States in 1933, he used this plan to help the entire

WHO'S WHO IN NEW YORK?

Langston Hughes (1902–1967) was a well-known poet who wrote about African-American life in the United States. He also wrote novels, short stories, and plays. Hughes lived in Harlem.

41

Desperate for cash, a man tries to sell his car in New York City during the Great Depression.

$100. WILL BUY THIS CAR MUST HAVE CASH LOST ALL ON THE STOCK MARKET

nation. These ideas that originated in New York State helped the country get through a very hard time.

WHO'S WHO IN NEW YORK?

Franklin Delano Roosevelt (1882–1945) was elected governor of New York in 1928. He led the state, and later the country, out of the Great Depression. He was elected as president to four terms, serving from 1933 until his death in 1945. He calmed a troubled nation with the words, "The only thing we have to fear is fear itself." Roosevelt was born in Hyde Park.

The Great Depression gradually came to an end with the start of World War II (1939–1945). In 1941, the United States entered the war to help France, Britain, and other countries fight against Germany. New York provided more war supplies than any other state. Fighter planes were made in Buffalo, guns came from Syracuse, and Rochester made periscopes and cameras. Companies across the nation made money from selling war supplies to the government. Once again, New York was able to grow.

POST-WAR

After World War II, the United States was ready for peace and stability. In 1952, the United Nations headquarters was built in New York City. This international organization was created to promote peace, understanding, and respect around the world. Their headquarters was a place where countries could settle their differences in a non-violent way. The United Nations continues this effort today.

In the 1950s, Levittown was considered the ideal American suburb.

Many World War II veterans and their families settled in Levittown, New York, just outside of New York City. Levittown had rows and rows of mass-produced, inexpensive homes. This kind of housing area was called a suburb, and it was copied all over the country.

Housing was not the only thing that expanded after the war. The Governor Thomas E. Dewey New York State Thruway was built during the 1950s. This superhighway stretches 641 miles (1,032 km) across New York State, making it the longest toll road in the United States. It connects the state's two largest cities—New York City and Buffalo. This highway made traveling upstate quicker and easier.

These expansion projects took land away from Iroquois reservations upstate. In the 1950s, the St. Lawrence Seaway was built between the Gulf of St. Lawrence and Lake Superior. The Seaway gave trading ships a direct route from the Great Lakes to the Atlantic Ocean, but it also took about 130 acres (53 ha) of land away from the St. Regis–Mohawk

FIND OUT MORE

Land claims are still an issue between the Iroquois and New York State. In October 2001, the Cayuga Indian Nation was awarded $248 million for the loss of its tribal lands due to an unfair treaty that was made with the state more than 200 years ago. Why did the Cayuga feel the treaty was unfair? How are other Iroquois tribes fighting for their land?

Reservation. Also, in 1961 the Niagara Power Project was built to harness the waterpower of Niagara Falls. When it was finished, 560 acres (227 ha) had been taken from the Tuscarora Indian Reservation to create a reservoir.

MODERN TIMES

In the 1970s and 1980s, jobs in manufacturing decreased by almost half-a-million. Demand for products was down, and some companies left for better locations. More than 680,000 New Yorkers left to find better job opportunities in other parts of the country. Many people moved from the cities out to the suburbs.

New York pushed for a cleaner environment in the 1980s. Love Canal, a neighborhood in Niagara Falls, was used as a toxic waste disposal site in the 1940s and 1950s. The waste-filled canal was filled in and given to the city of Niagara Falls. Homes and an elementary school were soon built. By the late 1970s, the dangerous chemicals began seeping out of the ground

A sign warns of hazardous waste contamination at a school in Love Canal.

and into the water. Studies found that the chemicals were responsible for the high rate of birth defects and cancer in this area. The situation was declared a national emergency and the people were evacuated.

New York was very successful during the 1990s. By the end of the decade, unemployment in New York State was cut nearly in half. Big companies like PepsiCo and IBM invested money in the state and created new jobs for New Yorkers.

In 2001 New York was in the national spotlight. On the morning of September 11, terrorists hijacked two commercial airliners and crashed them into the twin towers of the World Trade Center. Both towers collapsed, killing thousands of people. The same morning, two other planes were hijacked. One crashed into the Pentagon, near Washington, D.C., and the other, believed to be headed for the White House, went down in a field in Pennsylvania.

The World Trade Center was the heart of Manhattan's financial district and the largest commercial complex in the world. It was home to many banking and finance companies, government agencies, and international trade organizations. The towers had long symbolized our nation's strength and success.

Prior to September 11, 2001, the twin towers stood as a proud symbol of our country's economic power.

45

Mayor Giuliani was a strong leader for New York in the aftermath of September 11th.

The attack shocked not only the people of New York, but the entire country. Relief organizations like the Red Cross were flooded with donations. Volunteers came from all over the country to help in any way they could. New York City Mayor Rudolph W. Giuliani spoke to the grieving city at a prayer service in Yankee Stadium on September 23, 2001. He said, "Now we understand much more clearly why people from all over the globe want to come to New York, and to America. . . why they always have, and why they always will. It's called freedom, equal protection under law, respect for human life, and the promise of opportunity."

CHAPTER FOUR

GOVERNING NEW YORK

The government of New York is set up according to the constitution, a document that states the fundamental laws of a government. New York drafted its first constitution in 1777. Since then, it has adopted new constitutions in 1821, 1846, 1894, and 1938. New York has the opportunity to rewrite its constitution every 20 years. Amendments, or changes, may be made at any time.

New York's constitution divides the state government into three branches, or parts: the executive, the legislative, and the judicial. All three branches work together to make New York a safe and enjoyable place to live.

The magnificent capitol building is one of the highlights of Albany.

EXECUTIVE BRANCH

The executive branch enforces and carries out the laws of New York. The governor is head of the executive branch. He or she prepares the

EXTRA! EXTRA!

Four New York governors went on to serve as president of the United States: Martin Van Buren (1837–1841); Grover Cleveland (1885–1889 and 1893–1897); Theodore Roosevelt (1901–1909); and Franklin D. Roosevelt (1933–1945).

Lawmakers gather in the Assembly Chamber, the largest room in the capitol building.

budget, which determines how the state's money will be spent. The governor is also commander-in-chief of the state's military forces, and may call them to action in an emergency.

The governor is elected by the people to serve a four-year term. If the people think he or she is doing a good job, the governor may be re-elected for another four years. Other executive officers are the lieutenant governor, the attorney general, and the comptroller. These officers are also elected to four-year terms.

The Board of Regents and the secretary of state are also part of the executive branch. The Board of Regents is in charge of education in New York, and the secretary of state is in charge of the state departments, such as banking, education, health, and labor. The secretary of state is chosen by the governor. The officials on the Board of Regents are chosen by the legislature (New York's lawmaking body).

LEGISLATIVE BRANCH

The legislative branch makes new laws. There are two parts to the legislature: the senate and the assembly. New Yorkers elect 61 members of the senate and 150 members of the assembly. Senate and assembly members are elected for two-year terms.

NEW YORK STATE GOVERNMENT

EXECUTIVE BRANCH

Governor

Lieutenant Governor

Secretary of State

Board of Regents

Attorney General

Comptroller

Department Heads for:

Agriculture & Markets	Health
Banking	Insurance
Civil Service	Labor
Correctional Services	Lottery
Education	Motor Vehicles
Environmental	Social Services
Conservation	State
Family Assistance	Taxation
	Transportation

LEGISLATIVE BRANCH

Senate

Assembly

JUDICIAL BRANCH

Court of Appeals

Appellate Courts

Supreme Court

Court of Claims

County Courts

Family Courts

Surrogate Courts

The judicial branch interprets, or explains, the laws and makes sure they are fair. The New York court system makes up the judicial branch. When a person is accused of breaking a law, the case is taken to court. New York hears more than three million criminal and civil cases per year. Criminal cases involve breaking the law, and civil cases involve the violation of a person's rights.

The court of appeals is the highest, or most important, court in New York. An *appeal* is a request for a higher court to review a decision made in a lower court in order to determine if the decision was fair. To do this, the court of appeals will hear the case and either uphold the decision of the lower court, or overturn (reverse) it. The governor chooses six associate judges and one chief judge to serve a fourteen-year term on the court of appeals.

Below the court of appeals are the appellate divisions of the supreme court and the supreme court. The supreme court is divided into twelve judicial districts. Twelve supreme court justices are elected for fourteen-year terms. Some cases begin in the supreme court, and both courts hear appeals.

Other courts in New York include the court of claims, which hears cases that are made against the state of New York. Each county has a family court and surrogate court. If a child between the ages of eight and sixteen breaks the law, the case is heard in family court. This court also handles other family issues, including child custody and adoptions.

NEW YORK GOVERNORS

Name	Term	Name	Term
George Clinton	1777–1795	Alonzo B. Cornell	1880–1882
John Jay	1795–1801	Grover Cleveland	1883–1885
George Clinton	1801–1804	David B. Hill	1885–1891
Morgan Lewis	1804–1807	Roswell P. Flower	1892–1894
Daniel D. Tompkins	1807–1817	Levi P. Morton	1895–1896
John Tayler	1817	Frank S. Black	1897–1898
De Witt Clinton	1817–1822	Theodore Roosevelt	1899–1900
Joseph C. Yates	1823–1824	Benjamin B. Odell, Jr.	1901–1904
De Witt Clinton	1825–1828	Frank W. Higgins	1905–1906
Nathaniel Pitcher	1828	Charles E. Hughes	1907–1910
Martin Van Buren	1829	Horace White	1910
Enos T. Throop	1829–1832	John Alden Dix	1911–1912
William L. Marcy	1833–1838	William Sulzer	1913
William H. Seward	1839–1842	Martin H. Glynn	1913–1914
William C. Bouck	1843–1844	Charles S. Whitman	1915–1918
Silas Wright	1845–1846	Alfred E. Smith	1919–1920
John Young	1847–1848	Nathan L. Miller	1921–1922
Hamilton Fish	1849–1850	Alfred E. Smith	1923–1928
Washington Hunt	1851–1852	Franklin D. Roosevelt	1929–1932
Horatio Seymour	1853–1854	Herbert H. Lehman	1933–1942
Myron H. Clark	1855–1856	Charles Poletti	1942
John A. King	1857–1858	Thomas E. Dewey	1943–1954
Edwin D. Morgan	1859–1862	W. Averell Harriman	1955–1958
Horatio Seymour	1863–1864	Nelson A. Rockefeller	1959–1973
Reuben E. Fenton	1865–1868	Malcolm Wilson	1973–1974
John T. Hoffman	1869–1872	Hugh L. Carey	1975–1982
John Adams Dix	1873–1874	Mario M. Cuomo	1983–1994
Samuel J. Tilden	1875–1876	George E. Pataki	1995–2007
Lucius Robinson	1877–1879	Eliot Spitzer	2007–

Surrogate court handles wills and estates of those who have passed away. Each county also has a county court to hear criminal and civil cases.

Local courts also hear criminal and civil cases. These include the New York City civil and criminal courts, district courts in Nassau and Suffolk counties, city courts for areas outside New York City, and justice courts, which include town and village courts.

The interior of the capitol is especially beautiful. The lobby, shown here, has vaulted ceilings.

TAKE A TOUR OF ALBANY, THE STATE CAPITAL

Albany was one of the first Dutch settlements in New Netherland. In 1624, the Dutch West India Company set up the site as a fur-trading post and called it Fort Orange. Later, Fort Orange became known as Albany, after the Duke of York and Albany.

The centerpiece of Albany is the capitol building. It took four architects and 32 years to complete (1867–1899), but it was worth the wait. The capitol is a majestic building that stands five stories high. It is made mostly of gray granite.

Inside there are three main staircases. The Great West Staircase is the most magnificent. It is also called the Million Dollar Staircase because it cost more than $1 million to build. It has 444 steps and took 14 years to finish. The busts (sculptures of a person's head, neck, and shoulders) of 77 famous Americans, including George Washington, Abraham Lincoln, and Susan B. Anthony, are carved into the staircase.

The capitol is part of the Nelson A. Rockefeller Empire State Plaza. The plaza is a combination of government offices and a cultural center. Visitors can ride to the observation deck of the Corning Tower, relax among reflecting pools, or view the Empire State Art Collection. The New York State Museum, the largest state museum in the country, is also part of the plaza. There you'll find exhibits about state birds and minerals and the Adirondacks wilderness. There is also a replica of an Iroquois longhouse. Complete your plaza tour with a show or concert at the Empire State Performing Arts Center. It is often called the Egg because of its shape.

Fourth of July fireworks light up Empire State Plaza.

53

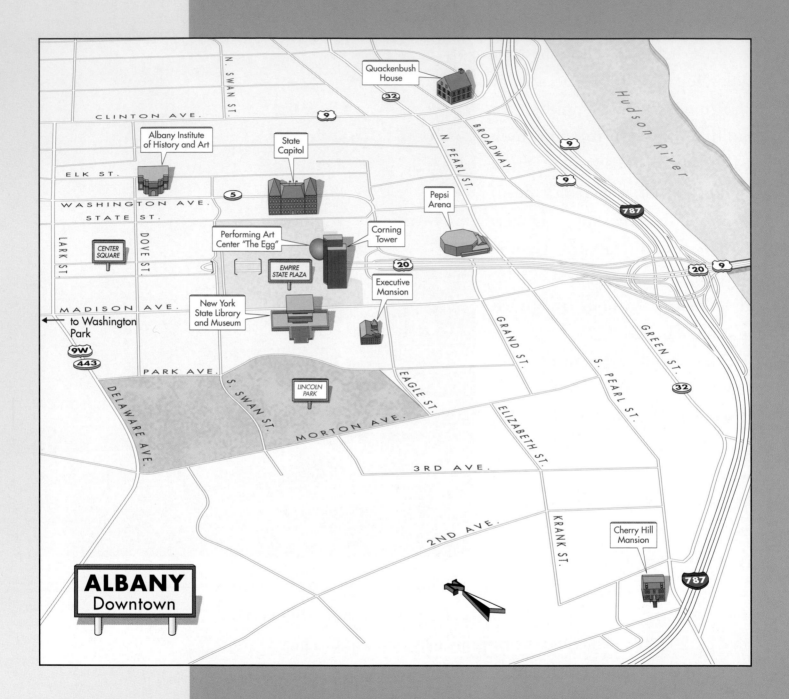

Quackenbush House

Albany Institute of History and Art

State Capitol

Pepsi Arena

Performing Art Center "The Egg"

Corning Tower

Executive Mansion

New York State Library and Museum

to Washington Park

EMPIRE STATE PLAZA

CENTER SQUARE

Cherry Hill Mansion

LINCOLN PARK

CLINTON AVE.

N. SWAN ST.

ELK ST.

WASHINGTON AVE.

STATE ST.

LARK ST.

DOVE ST.

MADISON AVE.

PARK AVE.

DELAWARE AVE.

S. SWAN ST.

MORTON AVE.

3RD AVE.

2ND AVE.

KRANK ST.

ELIZABETH ST.

EAGLE ST.

GRAND ST.

S. PEARL ST.

GREEN ST.

N. PEARL ST.

BROADWAY

Hudson River

ALBANY
Downtown

For three days at the start of spring, Albany celebrates its Dutch heritage with the Annual Tulip Festival. Most events take place in Washington Park, including picnics, entertainment, crafts, and the crowning of the Tulip Queen. If you can't make it to the park, you won't miss all the fun—the entire city is filled with more than 150,000 blooming tulips.

In the South End of Albany is Cherry Hill, a Gregorian-style house built in 1787. Five generations of the Rensselaer family lived there until 1963. Now a museum, the house has 30,000 pieces of history on display, including diaries, letters, receipts, books, and recipes. You can take a tour to get a close-up look at 175 years of life in Albany.

Don't forget to stop by Quackenbush House. It was built in 1736 and is the oldest Dutch building still standing in the city. It is also the site of the Visitors Center, where you can see a film about Albany's history and pick up a walking tour brochure of the city.

CHAPTER FIVE

THE PEOPLE AND PLACES OF NEW YORK

New York City is a melting pot of people from many backgrounds.

If you were to say hello to New York, you would be greeting almost 19 million people! Only California and Texas have a higher population. Many New Yorkers live in New York City, which has a population of about eight million. New York City is the largest city in the state.

New York has always been home to people of different races. In 1998, New York State welcomed almost 100,000 immigrants, most of whom settled in New York City. The largest groups coming to New York today are from the Dominican Republic, China, Jamaica, and Mexico. According to the 2000 census, 68 in every 100 New Yorkers are of European descent, and 16 in every 100 are African American. Fifteen out of 100 people are Hispanic, and almost 6 in every 100 are Asian. More than 82,000 New Yorkers are Native American. Of that group, more than 8,000 live on one of New York's eight reservations.

WORKING IN NEW YORK

Jobs in New York are as diverse as its people. Jobs are divided into two groups: goods and services. Industries that produce goods include manufacturing and agriculture. Industries that provide services include finance, communications, and tourism, among other things. Almost 8 in every 10 New Yorkers work in service industries.

Manufacturing

Nearly 800,000 New Yorkers work in industrial plants. They manufacture chemical products, machinery, computer and electronic equipment, and food products. Rochester and New York City are the state's leading manufacturing areas. If you have ever taken a picture or worn glasses, you have the people of Rochester to thank. The world's largest manufacturer of photographic equipment is Eastman Kodak Company, located in Rochester. Bausch & Lomb Inc., also in Rochester, makes lenses for glasses, contacts, and cameras.

New York is the nation's largest center of printing and publishing books, magazines, and newspapers. McGraw-Hill, the country's fourth largest printing and publishing company, is in New York City. New York has about 830 newspapers, including the *New York Times* and the *Wall Street Journal.* Both are published in New York City and are read by people around the world. Many magazines are also published in New York, including *Newsweek, Time, Sports Illustrated,* and *Consumer Reports.*

WHO'S WHO IN NEW YORK?

Gail Borden Jr. (1801–1874) patented the process of evaporating milk in 1856. Evaporated milk is regular milk with 60% of its water removed; it can last up to two years when sealed in a can. He founded a dairy company, now called Borden, Inc., which is still successful today. Borden was born in Norwich.

A dairy farmer in Cazenovia feeds his cows.

When you think of Pepsi or paper, think of Purchase. This city in upstate New York is home of the world's largest paper production company, International Paper, and the world headquarters of PepsiCo Inc. In Armonk, north of New York City in Westchester County, you'll find IBM, the world leader in computer and office equipment.

Agriculture

New York has about 35,000 farms. Of these, 6,000 are dairy farms. As one of the top milk producers in the country, it is easy to see why New York dairy farms provide nearly half of the state's farm income. Most dairy farms are in western and central New York, though a few are found to the north, and some are in the Hudson Valley.

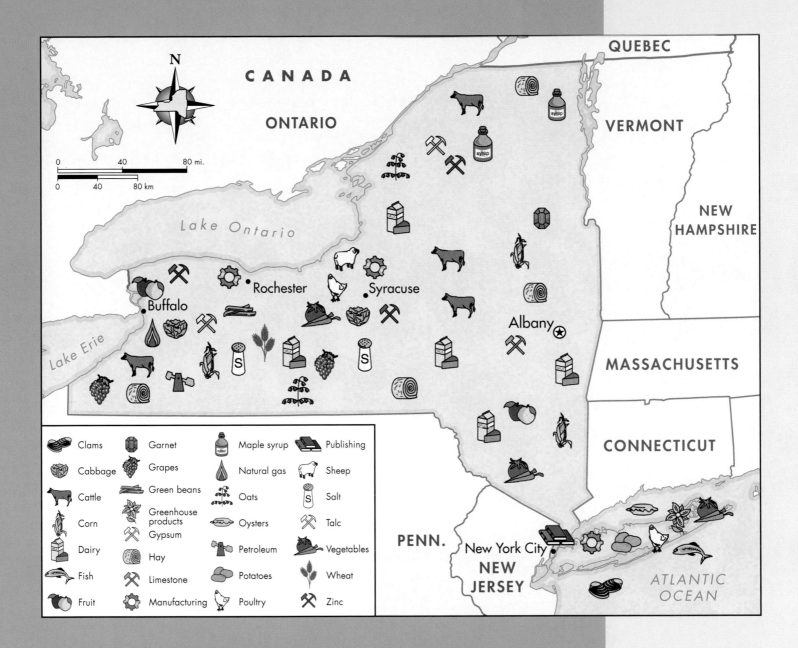

CANADA

ONTARIO

QUEBEC

VERMONT

NEW HAMPSHIRE

MASSACHUSETTS

CONNECTICUT

Lake Ontario

Lake Erie

Buffalo

Rochester

Syracuse

Albany

New York City

NEW JERSEY

PENN.

ATLANTIC OCEAN

N

0   40   80 mi.

0   40   80 km

Clams		Garnet		Maple syrup		Publishing
Cabbage		Grapes		Natural gas		Sheep
Cattle		Green beans		Oats		Salt
Corn		Greenhouse products		Oysters		Talc
Dairy		Gypsum		Petroleum		Vegetables
Fish		Hay		Potatoes		Wheat
Fruit		Limestone		Poultry		Zinc
		Manufacturing				

Apples are not only one of the state's most important products, they are also the state fruit. In 1987, the apple muffin became the state muffin when students at Bear Road Elementary School in North Syracuse started a petition in favor of the official state muffin. Remember to ask an adult for help!

OFFICIAL NEW YORK STATE APPLE MUFFINS

(makes 24 muffins)
2 c. flour
2 tsp. baking soda
1/2 c. sugar
1/8 tsp. nutmeg
3/4 c. brown sugar
1 1/2 tsp. cinnamon
1/2 tsp. salt

1/2 tsp. cloves
2 c. apples, coarsely chopped
1/2 c. raisins
1/2 c. walnuts, chopped
3 eggs
4 oz. cream cheese
1/2 c. butter, melted
1/2 tsp. vanilla

Topping:
1/2 c. walnuts, chopped
1/4 c. flour
1 tsp. lemon peel
1/2 c. brown sugar
1 tsp. cinnamon
1 oz. butter, melted

1. Preheat oven to 375°F.
2. In medium bowl, combine flour, baking soda, sugar, nutmeg, brown sugar, cinnamon, salt, and cloves. Set aside.
3. In large bowl, combine apples, raisins, walnuts, eggs, cream cheese, butter, and vanilla.
4. Add dry ingredients to apple mixture, a little at a time. Stir until just combined. Do not overmix.
5. Mix together the topping ingredients in a separate bowl.
6. Portion batter into muffin papers. Sprinkle with topping. Bake 20–30 minutes.
7. Serve with milk, the official beverage of New York State.

Two of New York's biggest crops are apples and grapes. Orchards and vineyards can be found in the fertile river valleys and lowlands surrounding the St. Lawrence, Hudson, and Mohawk Rivers, as well as Lakes Champlain, Erie, and Ontario. The sugar maple trees in the northern region produce maple syrup.

Service Industries

New York is a leader in many service industries, including finance, communications, and tourism. Five of the six largest banks in the United States have their headquarters in New York City. It is also the home of the New York Stock Exchange and the American Stock Exchange, the nation's first and second largest exchanges. New York City is the headquarters of NBC, CBS, and ABC, the country's three major television networks. The two largest phone companies in the nation, AT&T and Verizon, are both in New York City.

Travel and tourism is big business for New York, bringing in more than $22 billion per year. With New York's rich history, diverse people, and beautiful landscape, is it any wonder millions of people from all over the world visit the state? Let's take a tour of New York and see what all the fuss is about.

Stock traders on Wall Street scramble to buy and sell stocks

Western New York

Start your journey with the biggest splash in the state—Niagara Falls! It is one of the region's most breathtaking natural wonders. The falls are part of Niagara Reservation Park, the oldest state park in New York. You can pass directly in front of the falls on a *Maid of the Mist* tour. This tour boat service has been in operation since 1846.

Most of the 1.3 million people in the Greater Niagara region live in Buffalo. Sports fans root for the Bills, the city's professional football team, and the Sabres, its professional hockey team.

More than 270,000 people live in the heart of the Allegheny Mountains. So many Concord grapes are grown in this region that it is known as the grape juice capital of the world. This region is also home to the Seneca Nation of Indians, who live on the Allegheny, Cattaraugus, Old Springs, and Tonawanda Reservations. The Senecas were originally part of the Iroquois Confederacy. You can learn about their history at the Seneca-Iroquois National Museum in Salamanca.

Join the hundreds of thousands of people hiking, fishing, horseback riding, and skiing in Allegany State Park. Located in Cattaraugus County, it is New York State's largest state park. The park's 65,000 acres (26,305 ha) of forests, mountains, meadows, streams, and ponds attract nature lovers year-round.

Most of New York's concord grapes are used to make grape juice.

Central New York

In the Finger Lakes region you'll find the eleven Finger Lakes, Lake Ontario, and Taughannock Falls, a 215-foot (66-m) waterfall. Also in this region is the reservation of the Oneida Nation, one of the five original nations in the Iroquois Confederacy.

Most of the region's 1.9 million people live in the big cities of Rochester, Syracuse, and in the Corning/Elmira area. In Rochester you can tour the house that George Eastman built. Having made millions from his company, Eastman Kodak, Eastman spared no expense in creating his lavish home and gardens. Another famous home in the area is Harriet Tubman's house in Auburn.

The Central–Leatherstocking region is in the heart of the state, covering nine counties in the Mohawk Valley from the Catskills to the central Adirondacks. Author James Fenimore set most of his famous frontier tales in the Leatherstocking area in the late 19th century. The name comes from the leather stockings frontiersmen wore as they settled this region.

WHO'S WHO IN NEW YORK?

George Eastman (1854–1932) was an inventor and philanthropist. His inventions, especially the Brownie camera, made picture taking easy and inexpensive. With the great success of Eastman Kodak, he was able to donate money to several colleges in the United States, as well as in other countries. Eastman was born in Waterville.

WHO'S WHO IN NEW YORK?

James Fenimore Cooper (1789–1851) was one of America's first successful popular novelists. He created a character called Natty Bumppo in the *Leatherstocking Tales*, a classic collection of five tales about the American frontier. He lived in Cooperstown.

N

CANADA

QUEBEC

ONTARIO

Plattsburgh

Ausable
Chasm

VERMONT

ADIRONDACK
PARK

Watertown

87

Lake Ontario

Oswego

NEW
HAMPSHIRE

Saratoga
Springs

81

Niagara
Falls

Lewiston

Rochester

90

Utica

Saratoga
Spa S.P.

Buffalo

Geneva

Auburn

Syracuse

Cooperstown

Schenectady

Howe
Caverns

Hamburg

390

National Baseball
Hall of Fame

Albany

90

Lake Erie

Eden

FINGER LAKES
NATIONAL
FOREST

81

88

87

90

MASSACHUSETTS

Seneca-
Iroquois
National
Museum

Salamanca

86

ALLEGANY
STATE PARK

Corning

Elmira

CATSKILL
PARK

86

PENNSYLVANIA

Poughkeepsie

CONNECTICUT

84

West
Point

84

684

Long Island Sound

Yonkers

New York City

87

NEW
JERSEY

ATLANTIC OCEAN

State park or national forest

Highway

Capital city

City

State park (not all shown)

Tourist site

0   40   80 mi.

0   40   80 km

Cooperstown, founded by William Cooper in 1787, is home to the National Baseball Hall of Fame. The museum is dedicated to preserving the history of baseball. More than 30,000 baseball-related objects, including uniforms, player equipment, and ballpark artifacts, are on display.

In the 1800s, Syracuse was the nation's leading manufacturer of salt. It became known as Salt City. At the Salt Museum, you can see how people boiled salt water from Onondaga Lake in large kettles sunk into the floor.

The main road through Syracuse used to be part of the old Erie Canal system. Today, an old weighlock station, a place where boats were weighed as they traveled along the canal, houses the Erie Canal Museum in Syracuse. At the museum you can learn about the history of the canal, see a replica of an Erie steamship, and see what life was like along the canal.

One of the most interesting attractions in the Schoharie Valley is Howe Caverns. In 1842, a farmer named Lester Howe noticed his cows acting strangely. Instead of seeking shade from the hot sun, they clustered together in an open field. He discovered they were attracted to a cool breeze coming out of the ground, which turned out to be a hidden entrance to a cavern. Lester Howe explored the cavern and began to give tours. The first tours of Howe Caverns took eight to ten hours. Today

The Baseball Hall of Fame features exhibits on many famous players throughout history, including Babe Ruth and Ted Williams, shown here.

Although Saratoga Springs is well known for its healing waters, the downtown area also attracts many visitors.

you can explore these amazing mineral caves in about an hour.

Not far from Albany, you can relax and enjoy Saratoga Spa State Park, home of the famous mineral springs. During the Gilded Age, the rich and famous flocked to the area to relax in the soothing spas, which are still popular today. This 2,000-acre (810-ha) park also offers golfing in the summer and ice skating in winter.

Northern New York

In northern New York you'll find the Thousand Islands. Native Americans called this region *man-i-to-anna* which means, "The garden-place of the Great Spirit." According to Native American legend, the Great Spirit was carrying away paradise in a blanket. The blanket broke and paradise fell, breaking into a thousand pieces. Although it is called the Thousand Islands, there are actually between 1,500 and 1,900 islands that are home to more than 346,000 residents.

The Thousand Islands region includes the unfinished castle of George C. Boldt. Boldt was the owner of the famous Waldorf-Astoria hotel in New York City. In the early 1900s, he started building a 120-room mansion for his wife. Sadly, she died before it was finished, and he didn't have the heart to continue construction. Today you can take a tour of the castle, which includes information about the life of George and Louise Boldt.

The rugged beauty of the Adirondacks has attracted visitors since the 1800s. People come to hike and ski the mountain trails, and fish, swim, and sail on the region's 2,000 lakes. Rafting is popular along the Ausable River at the bottom of Ausable Chasm, a gorge with cliffs that rise 100 to 200 feet (30 to 61 m). It is one of the oldest tourist attractions in the United States. Much of the land in the Adirondacks is protected from development, but many people live and work in the area.

Southern New York

The Hudson Valley was home to some of New York's wealthiest residents during the Gilded Age. Kykuit was the home of the Rockefellers. Cornelius Vanderbilt's grandson, Frederick, built the Vanderbilt mansion. Other historic homes in the Hudson Valley include Springwood, home of Franklin D. Roosevelt, and Val-Kill, Eleanor Roosevelt's retreat house.

The United States Military Academy at West Point is about 50 miles (80 km) north of New York City, on the west shore of the Hudson River. Every year, more than 900 men and women graduate from the Academy

The Ausable River continues to carve out the gorge of Ausable Chasm.

West Point cadets march in full dress uniform.

to become officers in the United States Army. The Academy houses the oldest and largest public military collection in the Western Hemisphere.

Next let's go to New York City. More than ten and a half million people live in the city's five boroughs and the two counties of Long Island. In the Bronx, the northernmost borough, you'll find the Bronx Zoo, the largest city zoo in the United States. The zoo has more than 6,000 animals, including polar bears, red pandas, giraffes, snakes, seals, and many more. The Congo Gorilla Forest is home to 400 rain forest animals, including 22 gorillas. Across the street are the New York Botanical Gardens, the oldest and largest gardens in New York City. The gardens cover 250 acres (101 ha), including 50 acres (20 ha) of the forest that once covered all of New York.

Already world famous for its vast collection of dinosaur fossils, the latest addition to Manhattan's American Museum of Natural History is the Rose Center for Earth and Space. There you can explore the universe, learn about black holes, and walk a cosmic timeline. The museum is next to Central Park, located in the center of upper Manhattan. The park stretches 51 blocks between 59th and 110th streets. New Yorkers use it like a big backyard!

In the heart of Manhattan is Times Square, the center of New York's world-famous theater district. Enormous electric billboards advertise everything from shows to clothing to soft drinks. Thousands of people crowd its streets day and night.

No tour of New York would be complete without a ferry ride to Ellis Island. At the Ellis Island Immigration Museum, you can walk the same grounds as more than 12 million immigrants throughout history. This site was the main entry for people coming to the United States between 1892 and 1954.

As you can see, New York has it all! The state's rich history, varied landscape, and diverse population continue to make New York an exciting place to live and visit.

Times Square is sometimes called the Crossroads of the World because it attracts more than 27 million tourists each year.

NEW YORK ALMANAC

Statehood date and number: July 26, 1788/11th

State seal: Features a shield with trading ships sailing the Hudson River. On either side of the shield are two goddesses. To the left is Liberty. The crown at her feet symbolizes the victory of the American colonies over the British in the Revolutionary War. To the right is Justice. She is blindfolded and holds the scales of justice, which means that all citizens are equal in the eyes of the law. The state motto, Excelsior, is on a banner at the bottom of the seal. Adopted in 1882.

State flag: New York State coat of arms on a dark blue background. Adopted in 1778.

Geographic center: Madison County, approximately 12 miles (19 km) south of Oneida and 26 miles (42 km) southwest of Utica

Total area/rank: 54,556 square miles (141,299 sq km)/27th

Coastline: 127 miles (204 km)/14th

Borders: Connecticut, Massachusetts, New Jersey, Pennsylvania, the Atlantic Ocean, Vermont, Lake Erie, Lake Ontario, and Canada

Latitude and longitude: New York is located approximately between 40° 30' and 45° 00' N and 72° 10' and 79° 45' W.

Highest/lowest elevation: Mt. Marcy in the Adirondack region, 5,344 feet (1,629 m) above sea level/Atlantic coast, sea level

Hottest/coldest temperature: 108°F (42°C) in Troy on July 22, 1926/–52°F (–47°C) in Old Forge on February 18, 1979

Land area/rank: 41,274 square miles (122,283 sq km)/30th

Inland water area/rank: 1,895 square miles (4,908 sq km)/8th

Population/rank (2000 census): 18,976,457/3rd

Population of major cities:
New York City: 8,008,278
Buffalo: 292,648
Rochester: 219,773
Yonkers: 196,086
Syracuse: 147,306
Albany: 95,658

Origin of state name: Named for the Duke of York in 1664, when the British took New Netherland from the Dutch

Capital: Albany

Previous capitals: Kingston (1777–1789), New York City (1789–1797)

Counties: 62

State government: 61 senators, 150 representatives

Major rivers/lakes: St. Lawrence, Hudson, Mohawk, Genesse, Allegheny, Susquehanna, Delaware/Lake Champlain, Lake Ontario, Oneida Lake, Lake Erie, Lake George, Finger Lakes

Farm products: Milk, cheese, apples, grapes, wine, strawberries, cherries, pears, onions, potatoes, cabbage, sweet corn, green beans, cauliflower, field corn, hay, wheat, oats, maple syrup, and dry beans

Manufactured products: Books and periodicals, clothing and apparel, pharmaceuticals, machinery, instruments, toys and sporting goods, electronic equipment, automotive and aircraft components

Mining products: Crushed stone, portland cement, salt, sand and gravel, and zinc

Fishing products: Clams, lobsters, crabs, bass, catfish, trout, and salmon

Animal: Beaver

Beverage: Milk

Bird: Bluebird

Fish: Brook trout and striped bass

Flower: Rose

Fossil: *Eurypterus remipes*

Fruit: Apple

Gem: Garnet

Insect: Ladybug

Motto: Exelsior ("Ever Upward")

Muffin: Apple muffin

Nicknames: The Empire State, the Knickerbocker State

Shell: Bay Scallop

Song: "I Love New York"

Tree: Sugar maple

Wildlife: White-tailed deer, red foxes, black bears, skunks, raccoons, beavers, opossums, squirrels, woodchucks, woodpeckers, sparrows, hawks, crows, goldfinches, crabs, bluefish, trout, lobsters, crabs, sharks, and whales

TIMELINE

NEW YORK STATE **HISTORY**

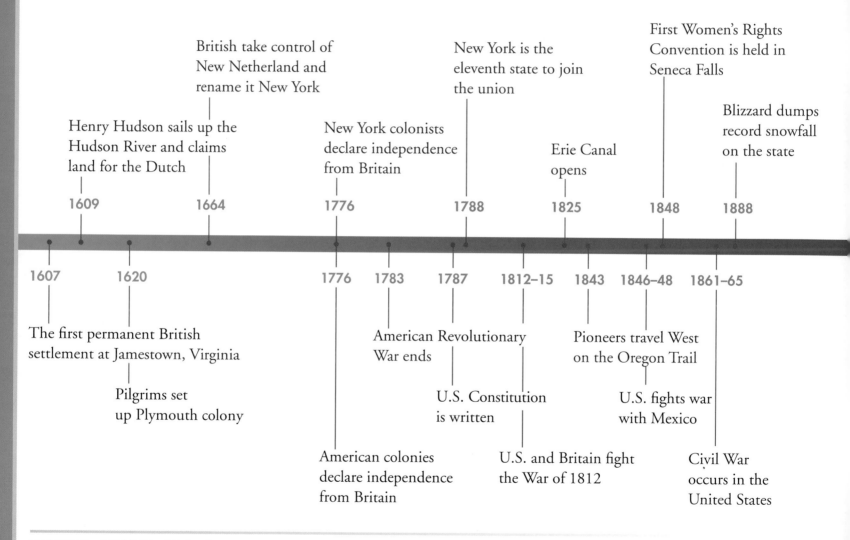

British take control of
New Netherland and
rename it New York

Henry Hudson sails up the
Hudson River and claims
land for the Dutch

New York is the
eleventh state to join
the union

First Women's Rights
Convention is held in
Seneca Falls

New York colonists
declare independence
from Britain

Erie Canal
opens

Blizzard dumps
record snowfall
on the state

1609　　　1664　　　1776　　　1788　　　1825　　　1848　　　1888

1607　　1620　　　1776　1783　1787　1812–15　1843　1846–48　1861–65

The first permanent British
settlement at Jamestown, Virginia

American Revolutionary
War ends

Pioneers travel West
on the Oregon Trail

Pilgrims set
up Plymouth colony

U.S. Constitution
is written

U.S. fights war
with Mexico

American colonies
declare independence
from Britain

U.S. and Britain fight
the War of 1812

Civil War
occurs in the
United States

UNITED STATES **HISTORY**

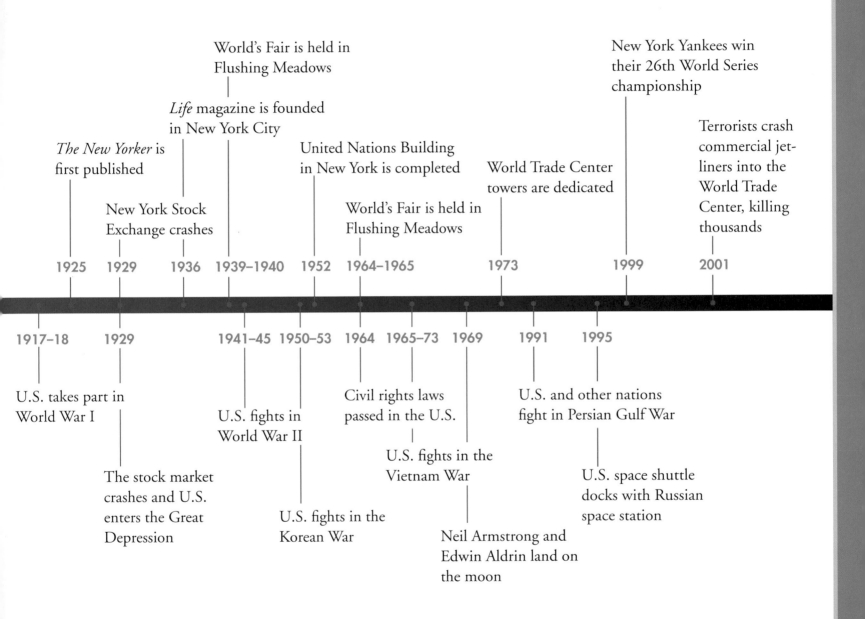

World's Fair is held in
Flushing Meadows

Life magazine is founded
in New York City

The New Yorker is
first published

New York Stock
Exchange crashes

United Nations Building
in New York is completed

World's Fair is held in
Flushing Meadows

World Trade Center
towers are dedicated

New York Yankees win
their 26th World Series
championship

Terrorists crash
commercial jet-
liners into the
World Trade
Center, killing
thousands

1925   1929   1936   1939–1940   1952   1964–1965   1973   1999   2001

1917–18   1929   1941–45   1950–53   1964   1965–73   1969   1991   1995

U.S. takes part in
World War I

The stock market
crashes and U.S.
enters the Great
Depression

U.S. fights in
World War II

U.S. fights in the
Korean War

Civil rights laws
passed in the U.S.

U.S. fights in the
Vietnam War

Neil Armstrong and
Edwin Aldrin land on
the moon

U.S. and other nations
fight in Persian Gulf War

U.S. space shuttle
docks with Russian
space station

73

GALLERY OF FAMOUS NEW YORKERS

Shirley Chisholm
(1924–2005)
First African-American woman elected to the United States Congress in 1969. Born in Brooklyn.

Ella Fitzgerald
(1917–1996)
Famous singer who recorded more than 2,000 songs and won 13 Grammy awards, including one for Lifetime Achievement. Grew up in Yonkers and lived in Harlem.

Ruth Bader Ginsburg
(1933–)
The second woman (after Sandra Day O'Connor) to sit as a United States Supreme Court Justice, in 1993. Born in New York City.

Madeleine L'Engle
(1918–2007)
Well-loved children's book author. She received the 1963 Newbery Medal for *A Wrinkle in Time*. Born in New York City.

Carolyn McCarthy
(1944–)
United States Congresswoman representing Long Island. She was first elected to the United States House of Representatives in 1996 and was reelected in 1998 and 2000. A lifelong resident of Mineola.

Colin Powell
(1937–)
Highest-ranking African-American officer in United States history. In 2001 he was selected by President George W. Bush to become secretary of state, making him the first African American to hold this office. Born in New York City.

Tito Puente
(1923–2000)
Bandleader, composer, arranger, and percussionist. Puente was known as "El Rey," the King of Mambo. He recorded 100 albums, published more than 400 compositions, and won 4 Grammy awards. Born in Spanish Harlem, New York City.

Maurice Sendak
(1928–)
Caldecott medal-winning illustrator and author of many classic children's books, including *Where the Wild Things Are*. Born in Brooklyn.

GLOSSARY

abolish: to get rid of something

abolitionist: a person who spoke out to end slavery

cadets: students at a military school

canal: an artificial waterway or artificially improved river used for travel, shipping, or irrigation

constitution: a system of fundamental laws of a government

democracy: government by the people, ruled by leaders who are chosen by the people

economy: a system of money management in a country, city, or community

era: an important period of time

estuary: the wide part of a river where it nears the sea, and fresh and salt water mix

glacier: a huge mass of ice

gorge: a deep and narrow ditch with high, rocky sides

immigrant: someone who travels from one country to another to live

legend: a story about the past that has not been proven true

magma: the fiery material under Earth's crust that turns to rock when it cools

plateau: a high, level, stretch of land, like a tabletop

repealed: canceled or reversed

suburb: a residential area just outside of a city

trade: buying and selling things in order to make a profit

treaty: agreement

tributary: a stream that flows into another body of water

veteran: person who has served in the armed forces

FOR MORE INFORMATION

Web sites

NYS Department of State Kids' Room

http://www.dos.state.ny.us/kidsroom/menupg.html
Facts about New York and information about the state symbols.

New-York Historical Society

http://www.nyhistory.org
Information about New York City history for children.

Official New York State Tourism Website

http://www.iloveny.com/
Information about attractions and events in New York.

Books

Fazio, Wende. *Times Square* (Cornerstones of Freedom). Danbury, CT: Children's Press, 1999.

Jacobs, William Jay. *Ellis Island: New Hope in a New Land*. New York, NY: Atheneum, 1990.

Lourie, Peter. *Erie Canal: Canoeing America's Great Waterway*. Honesdale, PA: Boyds Mills Press, 1997.

Sherrow, Victoria. *The Triangle Factory Fire*. Brookfield, CT: Millbrook Press, 1995.

Whitehurst, Susan. *The Colony of New York*. New York, NY: Rosen Publishing Group, 2000.

Addresses

Governor Eliot Spitzer
State Capitol
Albany, NY 12224

New York State Museum
Room 3023
Cultural Education Center
Albany, NY 12230

INDEX

ABOUT THE AUTHOR

Kristin Cotter was born in the Bronx. She graduated from New York's Fordham University, and has lived in New York's Rockland and Westchester counties. For this book, much of the research was done at the library and historical associations. The Internet was also an important tool, as was touring the state. Kristin is an assistant editor for a magazine, as well as a freelance writer. This is her first book for children.

Photographs © 2008: Brown Brothers: 26; Corbis Images: 37, 42 top, 43, 58 left, 63, 74 left (Bettmann), 46 (Mitchell Gerber), 74 bottom right (Ira Nowinski), 44 (Galen Rowell), 74 top right (Joseph Sohm/ChromoSohm Inc.), 39 (Underwood & Underwood), 31, 41; David J. Forbert: 65; Dembinsky Photo Assoc./Willard Clay: 3 left, 11; Envision/Henry T. Kaiser: 56; Getty Images: 40 (Archive Photos), 22, 34 (Hulton Archive), 61 (Roger Tully); Image State: 66 (Andre Jenny), cover (David Noton Photography), 45 (Johnny Stockshooter), 3 right, 69 (Chuck Szymanski); MapQuest.com, Inc.: 70 left; North Wind Picture Archives: 21, 28, 29, 30, 38; Photo Researchers, NY: 7 (Michael P. Gadomski), 15 (Rafael Macia); Robertstock.com: 18 (H. Abernathy), 10 (Camerique), 67 (P. Degginger), 53 (R. Krubner), 35; Stock Montage, Inc.: 20, 23, 24, 33, 36, 42 bottom; Superstock, Inc.: 9; The Image Works: 62 (Kirk Condyles), 48 (Howard Dratch), 58 bottom (Bob Mahoney), 68 (Mulvehill), 47, 49 background (Lee Snider), 16 (Ted Spiegel); Unicorn Stock Photos/Jeff Greenberg: 4; Viesti Collection, Inc.: 19 (Martha Cooper), 17 , 70 right (Bill Terry); Visuals Unlimited: 71 left (Steve Callahan), 13, 52 (Mark E. Gibson), 71 top right (Maslowski), 71 bottom right (Henry W. Robinson).

MINERAL COUNTY LIBRARY
PO BOX 1390
HAWTHORNE, NV 89415